Contents

Hat Hunt

These five hats have been hidden somewhere in your Annual. Jot down the pages where you spot them.

A BRIEF HISTORY OF SKYLANDS

Greetings, Portal Master! I am Eon, and it is my pleasure to welcome you to this special Skylanders Annual. Skylands has been my home for more years than I care to remember. It is a magical place, full of wonder and excitement. No one is quite sure of its true origins, but here are some of the key moments in Skylands history.

Long, long, long, long ago . . .

The universe springs into being and with it, Skylands – an infinite realm of floating islands. From here, you can travel anywhere in the cosmos: backwards, forwards, sideways and – according to some – even diagonally in time.

Long, long, long ago . . .

Evil tries to muscle its way into Skylands. The Darkness sweeps across the islands, bringing with it evil wizards, evil witches and even evil window cleaners. These are dark days. Literally. Pitch black. You can't see your beard in front of your face.

Long, long ago . . .

The Benevolent Ancients build the Core of Light to keep the Darkness at bay. Some say they only wanted a light so they could read in bed, but I have my doubts.

Long ago . . .

Huge robots known as the Arkeyans rise to power, after discovering how to combine the mystic Elements of Magic and Tech. They are a kindly race, concerned only with the pursuit of knowledge – until their leaders are tempted to follow the path of the Darkness. Corrupted by a new hunger for power, the Arkeyan Empire spreads throughout Skylands, enslaving every living soul (and quite a few undead ones too!).

This book belongs to . . .

Jake, Josh Mummy and Daddy

Published by Puffin 2014
A Penguin Company
Penguin Books Ltd, 80 Strand, London, WC2R 0RL, UK
Penguin Group (USA) Inc., 375 Hudson Street, New York 10014, USA
Penguin Books Australia Ltd, 707 Collins Street, Melbourne, Victoria 3008,
Australia (a division of Pearson Australia Group Pty Ltd)
Canada, India, New Zealand, South Africa

Written by Cavan Scott
Stories illustrated by Dani Geremia – Beehive Illustration Agency
Comic illustrated by Diego Diaz

www.puffinbooks.com

ISBN: 978–0–141–35134–6
001
Printed in China

10,000 years ago . . .

Tired of Arkeyan tyranny, a group of powerful Portal Masters gather the Giants, the first ever Skylanders. They defeat the Arkeyan King, but the Giants are accidentally transported to a small, blue-green planet called Earth.

The Portal Masters protect Skylands for millennia, assisted valiantly by generations of brave Skylanders. It is a golden age of peace and prosperity.

100 years ago . . .

The forces of Darkness attempt to sabotage the Mount Cloudbreak Eruption Ceremony. They are forced back by a special group of Skylanders – the SWAP Force. Unfortunately, the SWAP Force themselves are whisked away to Earth. What is it about your world, anyway?

4 years ago . . .

A foul little Portal Master by the name of Kaos destroys the Core of Light. I am reduced to a mere phantom and my Skylanders are banished to – well, you can guess, can't you? Darkness descends across our realm and Kaos reigns supreme. Until, that is, you discover the Skylanders and return them home. Kaos is vanquished and a second golden age begins. In fact, it's even shinier than the first – positively gleaming.

Did you know?

Every 100 years, Mount Cloudbreak erupts, distributing magic across Skylands' many islands.

BUT WHAT OF THE FUTURE?

No one knows – except for Octavius the Oracle and he's staying tight-lipped, the old spoilsport. Needless to say, the Darkness never gives up – but neither do you! Skylands will be safe for as long as you and your Skylanders are ready for action!

WHO'S YOUR SKYLANDER?

Ever wondered what kind of Skylander you'd be? Answer these questions to find out.

1. **You Portal into a Mabu town to find Chompy Powerhouses running amok. What do you do?**

A) Make sure you get the Mabu to safety first. You can deal with those pesky Chompies later.
B) Call down a shower of stars to defeat the minions, and then sweep away without saying a word.
C) Lose your temper and blast every Chompy in town. OK, so most of the town gets incinerated too, but those Chompies make you so MAD!
D) Grin as you leap into battle. At least life isn't boring!

2. **What do you like to do in your spare time?**

A) Help those who are less fortunate than yourself.
B) You're not telling. It's a secret.
C) Argue, mainly.
D) Go travelling. There's so much of the big wide world out there that you haven't seen.

3. **One of your fellow Skylanders accidentally blasts you in the rear end in the middle of a battle. Do you . . .**

A) Ignore it. You need to concentrate on the enemy, or someone might get hurt.
B) Glare at them and then sweep away without saying a word.
C) Lose your rag. What's wrong with these people?
D) Laugh it off. These things happen. It's all part of the fun.

4. **Do you like having a lot of friends?**

A) Yes. You always look after your mates.
B) No. You're a bit of a loner.
C) Until they annoy you, yes.
D) As long as they live life to the full, that's all right with you.

5. **Flynn is trapped in the bottom of a deep, dark pit. What do you do?**

A) Dive in and help him, of course. What other choice is there?
B) Creep down and appear behind him in the dark. Then, after rescuing the puffed-up pilot, sweep away without saying a word.
C) Oh well, you suppose you're going to have to rescue him. Why does he get himself into these scrapes?
D) Leap into the pit. You'd been meaning to see what's down there anyway.

6. **Where do you like going on holiday?**

A) Somewhere you can help people.
B) Somewhere remote.
C) Somewhere hot.
D) Somewhere there are loads of places to explore.

Wish you were here...

7. Your friends throw you a surprise birthday party. How do you react?

A) Make sure that everyone gets to have a slice of cake.
B) Nod your appreciation, and then sweep away without saying a word.
C) Have a great time, but secretly fume that there are people there who you can't stand! Have they come along just to wind you up?
D) Jump in and have a whale of a time. There are going to be party games, right?

8. What's your favourite type of food?

A) Anything you can share.
B) That's nobody else's business!
C) Curry. The hotter the better.
D) You don't know. You just like trying as many new things as possible.

9. It's the annual Skylander Battle Cry Contest and your turn has been skipped. What do you do?

A) Sit back and enjoy the rest of the show. It doesn't matter.
B) Give the referee a good hard stare, and then sweep away without saying a word.
C) Totally lose your rag, and shout so loud that no one else can be heard anyway!
D) Shrug it off. There are plenty of other things to be getting on with anyway.

10. What kind of stories do you like best?

A) Whatever other people like read to them.
B) Mysteries and thrillers.
C) What is it with all these questions?
D) Action adventures.

HOW DID YOU DO?

Mostly **A**s:
You are protective like
Bumble Blast

Mostly **B**s:
You are mysterious like
Star Strike

Mostly **C**s:
You are hot-headed like
Eruptor

Mostly **D**s:
You are adventurous like
Scratch

HEAD GAMES

by Onk Beakman

PART ONE: THE PETRIFIED FOREST

"Can't this thing go any faster?" complained Scorp. Behind the wheel of the Dread-Yacht, Flynn chuckled.

"Hold on to your pincers, Scorp old buddy. We're already travelling four times the speed of awesome. The new-improved Dread-Yacht is the fastest ship in all of Skylands."

Beside Scorp, Spyro paced up and down. He could understand the Earth Skylander's frustration. They were heading to the Weird Woods, an island hidden behind an ocean of thick storm clouds. Not even Eon could Portal them through such heavy cloud cover. Flynn was doing the best he could, but no ship was as fast as a Portal. Not even the Dread-Yacht.

"I'm sure we'll be there in plenty of time," said Wind-Up, peering over the side of the ship, watching for a break in the clouds.

"Yeah," chipped in Flynn. "Those Ent guys only called for help half an hour ago, anyhoo."

"Thirty-six minutes and forty-two seconds ago, to be exact," Wind-Up corrected. The small Tech Skylander was big on time-keeping.

"We'll be there with time to spare," Flynn insisted. "Just relax and enjoy the ride."

The Dread-Yacht bucked as Flynn narrowly avoided a sudden burst of lightning. "Sorry about that!"

Scorp clicked his claws together. "But if we're too late . . ."

"We won't be!" Spyro snapped, a little too forcibly. He was as concerned as the Sting Ball player. Eon had summoned them as soon as the call was heard. A group of Ent explorers had come under attack from the forces of the Darkness. Worst of all, Baron von Shellshock was involved.

"Who knows what that crab clown is doing down there?" growled Scorp, his stinger flexing in anticipation.

"Well, we're about to find out," yelled Flynn. "Land ahoy!"

The clouds parted to reveal an island covered in lush, purple trees.

"We're coming in too fast," shouted Wind-Up as the ground rushed up to meet them.

"Don't sweat it," said Flynn, looking from control to control. "Now, where did I put the brakes?"

Seconds later, the Dread-Yacht was on the ground. Actually, scratch that. The Dread-Yacht was pretty much *in* the ground, having carved a deep furrow in the forest floor.

"Textbook landing," Flynn boasted as they jumped down from the deck. "Sometimes I even impress myself."

Before Spyro could answer, an Ent burst from the undergrowth.

"Oh, th-th-thank the Benevolents," he stammered, wringing his wooden hands together. "It's t-t-terrible. The expedition is ruined."

"Where's Shellshock?" rumbled Scorp, ready for action. "He's got an appointment with my sting."

"Th-th-this way," the Ent gestured, leading them back into the trees. "Please, hurry."

***

"So you found an underground forest?" asked Spyro as they raced together down a long, dark mineshaft.

"Th-that's right," replied the terrified Ent, who had finally introduced himself as Worrywood. "And you'll never guess what grows on the branches."

"Petrified Darkness," gasped Wind-Up, as they turned a corner and entered a giant cavern. Twisted black trees were everywhere, jutting out of every rock and wall, glistening purple jewels hanging from their branches like fruit. Greebles were harvesting the crystals, the rest of Worrywood's expedition tied up in a clearing in the middle of the cavern. Spyro frowned. Shellshock's master – their archenemy Kaos – used Petrified Darkness to evilize innocent victims. Even the purest heart could be turned to the Darkness if struck by a beam from one of the purple gems.

"But where's the walking crab salad?" Flynn asked as he looked around for evidence of Baron von Shellshock.

Just then, a rasping voice echoed around the chamber. "Schnell, schnell you diddy dummkopfs."

"That answer your question?" Scorp hissed, glowing sting balls appearing in his claws.

"Where do you keep those things?" Flynn said, his eyes widening as he took in the slimy orbs. "On second thoughts, I don't want to know."

"Vot are you vaiting for?" Shellshock scuttled into the clearing, a huge staff in his claws. "Ve have to be avay before Eon's Skyschniztels arrive!"

"Too late, Baron," Spyro roared as the Skylanders broke cover, charging into battle. "Let's do this!"

"Defend ze crystals!" Shellshock shrieked, the Greebles behind him almost running into each other to grab their weapons.

"Defend yourself!" Scorp yelled back, lobbing a sticky emerald orb into the mob. The gem detonated, sending giggling Greebles flying everywhere.

"Time to get you out of here," said Wind-Up, rushing to the bound explorers and slicing through their ropes with sparking claws.

Spyro, meanwhile, had his own claws full with a gaggle of Greeble Screwballs. He leapt into the air, narrowly missing a twisting missile. "Flynn!" he yelled over his wings. "Get those Ents out of here. We need Wind-Up's help."

Flynn visibly gulped, his toothy grin faltering. "I thought I'd just cover the exit, you know? Just in case their reinforcements arrived?"

"Flynn!" Spyro barked.

"OK, OK," Flynn gave in, hurrying over to the explorers. "Keep your horns on."

Spyro roared out a column of flame, blasting a path through the Greebles. "Where are you, Shellshock?" the dragon yelled. "Scared of a little fire?"

"Baron von Shellshock iz scared of nothing!" the crab crowed, leaping forward, his crystal-tipped staff pointing straight at Spyro. "But you should be afraid of ze dark!"

A stream of dark indigo light shot from the Petrified Darkness and slammed into Spyro. The dragon bellowed helplessly.

"Don't you see, Spyro? Petrified Darkness, it can Evilize anyone – even a Skylander!"

"Woah, that's not good," gasped Flynn as Spyro started to change, the dragon's eyes flashing purple.

"No!" bellowed Spyro. "It's bad. Very bad – and it feels GREAT!"

Oh no!
Has Spyro
been Evilized?
Turn to page 50
to find out!

The Skylanders'

The Skylanders are brave, but they also know when to accept help from their friends. Here's a shout out to some of their finest allies . . .

10. WHEELLOCK

First seen in Skylanders SWAP Force

The 'long teeth of the law' in Iron Jaw Gulch, Marshall Wheellock helped the Skylanders defeat a swashbuckling band of Pirate Greebles. The sharp-shooting Dirt Shark now divides his time between maintaining law and order, and helping train the Skylanders in Woodburrow.

9. SOFTPAW

First seen in Skylanders SWAP Force

Special Agent 321 can infiltrate any top-secret base. He's also good at getting into less-secret places too, come to think of it. This wily fox always has a disguise or gadget ready, such as the 'Scout Hazards to Elude and Escape Poncho' (or S.H.E.E.P., for short).

8. THE HIPBROS

First seen in Skylanders SWAP Force

Gorm and Tuk are always on hand to help in Woodburrow. Bodybuilder Gorm works hard to keep his body in peak condition, while his easily annoyed brother Tuk is more concerned with making a quick buck in his Emporium. It takes all sorts.

7. SHARPFIN

First seen in Skylanders SWAP Force

The Baron of Motleyville, Sharpfin is always on the look-out for junk that he can transform into amazing machines. His rivals claim that he would sell his own granny to make a quick profit. This is unfair – he'd probably try to sell yours first.

6. AVRIL

First seen in Skylanders SWAP Force

The youngest of 12 children, this young Frost Elf was never taken seriously until she cleaned up at the annual Boney Islands Snowbrawl contest. Her tribe were so impressed they immediately elevated her to Captain of the Guard. Go Avril!

Top 10 Friends

5. PERSEPHONE

First seen in Skylanders Spyro's Adventure
This fairy queen has long been a friend of the Skylanders, offering power upgrades in exchange for treasures. She even stowed away on the Dread-Yacht when Flynn set sail to help find the Iron Fist of Arkus with the newly-returned Giants.

4. TESSA

First seen in Skylanders SWAP Force
The new chieftess of Woodburrow. When the Cloudbreak Islands were overrun by Greebles, plucky Tessa leapt onto her giant bird Whiskers and flew off to find help. She found Flynn, which was the next best thing. Working with the Skylanders, she helped save the Mount Cloudbreak Eruption Day celebrations. Often says 'Ka-Blam' when excited – which happens a lot.

3. HUGO

First seen in Skylanders Spyro's Adventure
For years, short-sighted Hugo was Master Eon's right-hand Mabu. Surviving the destruction of the Core of Light, the jittery librarian proved his worth by helping the Skylanders gather the Elemental Sources to defeat Kaos. Even though he'd rather put his feet up with a mug of steaming seaweed tea (his favourite) and a dusty old book, Hugo has the heart of a hero beating in that nervous little chest.

2. CALI

First seen in Skylanders Spyro's Adventure
One of Skylands' greatest explorers, Cali set out to map every single island before she was forced to give up after number 4,367. She settled in Eon's ruins, where she helped train the Skylanders. She never lost her adventurous streak – or her knack for getting captured. Recently, she was abducted by the Lord of the Underworld, Count Moneybone, and turned into a member of the Undead. Thankfully, she's back to normal now – although she has been known to howl at the moon every now and then (which is impressive as Skylands doesn't even have moons!).

1. FLYNN

First seen in Skylanders Spyro's Adventure
He may be conceited beyond belief, but Skylands' best pilot is never backwards in coming forwards – especially when evil is afoot. He flies his beloved Dread-Yacht into danger without question (or much of a clue, for that matter), ready to risk everything to help the Skylanders defeat followers of the Darkness. Of course, he largely thinks that the Skylanders are helping him, but who are we to put him right? Not that he'd listen anyway. BOOM!

CHOMPY

Look at this massive collection of Skylanders! Any minion would have to be crazy to hang around here – and it seems there are ten Chompies who fit the bill! Can you find the ten Chompies hiding on this spread?

SPOTTING

The Skylanders are always bellowing their battle cries as they jump through a Portal. You just can't stop 'em. Can you work out the missing words in the catchphrases below and then find them on the grid opposite?

Bouncer: "Deal with the _____ !"
Bumble Blast: "The _____ Swarm!"
Camo: "_____ Punch!"
Chill: "Stay _____"
Chop Chop: "_____ and Dice!"
Cynder: "Volts and _____ !"
Drobot: "Blink and _____ !"

"Blast and Fyhy pye!"

Blast Zone

Battle Cry
Bonanza

"_____ it Cool!"

Dune Bug: "Can't Beat the _____ !"
Eruptor: "_____ to Burn!"
Flashwing: "Bcinded by the Light!"
Free Ranger: "Whip Up a _____!"
Fright Rider: "Fear the _____ !"
Ghost Roaster: "No _____, No Gain!"
Gill Grunt: "_____ the Fish!"

"Let's Roll !"

Freeze Blade

Hot Dog: "See _____ Burn!"
Magna Charge: "_____ to Attack!"
Ninjini: "Any Last _____ ?"
Pop Fizz: "_____ of the Potion!"
Pop Thorn: "_____ to the Point!"
Prism Break: "The Beam is _____ !"
Scratch: "The _____ of the Claw!"

Roller Brawl

18

Slam Bam: *"Armed and _____!"*
Slobber Tooth: *"_____ and Slobber!"*
Smolderdash: *"A Blaze of _____!"*
Spy Rise: *"It's _____!"*
Spyro: *"All _____ Up!"*

Scorp

```
B I G J R O P N E Q V V O W G K G M T M R Z X R B N E H A K
J O B G N I D E E F I C F T S M F G C C D B L K O U C V C H
R U R U Z D Z P O M Z Y S U G R A E S T E P T I H X A E T C
L T J N X K U R Z O T O B N D P Z I X T Y F T W K C R X J Z
Z P I S U O I R U F D R S I L E N T Y Q S O R I I W B F D A
G E E P Z B K D O S A T E I B H M Q M Z M A U E U S X O N A
C L A S S I F I E D N S S L W N O T D B E N O F P R T Y N V
G A B H C X Z Y F V G E I I T U K X V V U A J T E Y F S D L
Q R V A E K S I S U E D A L N E C O O L F L T C Y Y M R K A
Y D M P U W H W N N R Z X G C W E S X A W D L T C Q X F W H
J L Q L K S S N E J O E X L N V N B X W J O W P R Y D V S U
S O O R E B S G R B U F O M B A H N L T P D Z F J A Q K T L
P G T C O S X F L L S B W G C U H N O K E E P I N G C M I Z
K I K Z H I P L D F B X D V K P M P D J D S Y C B Y L T N I
G T B O U Y D H I E Q E E C E R H R N N K X I Z U V Q W G A
X H K V I E R L R G L K V S O A E N E L R X K P W O A K N K
C Q Z Y D H X X F A H R W T V A N K X I D V S T M X K K U O
T K T N V T M U C P H T S J S F A H Z F X W N Z R S W Z J H
S U I M S G T S C S F I N C N P T C G A N I X D C E B I G Y
H L X C E J E I X F S N P I I J U S P E A R A S P H L L O R
B C A M H L B I U T Z J D M N U R L E E H W I U I S Q I E U
U O N P G A G P R L F Y U R Q G E U K S W B P P D I Y F G Z
D R E G R L I A T T K A C W S I R X O C P V D R R W H P O K
M I A Q O Q I N L P Q O I E G S Z Y C F W V E E T D N T J S
J N U R L G D Y P L B I L E C H O Y E N K U W M Y V L M P R
S J Y X H H A I I H H O F C D E R I F U H C K E D V M O B N
T U I T S S L W U Q A R E I R F C J P T V D U H R H T Q O Y
J X Q E M I A F C D O I A L L B U P F O G P H L E A T Z G Z
V B H E J H C F E A D O R S E G K E M I O M E O F A O P M H
Y I B E K T M D L M B D R H J I F O C W Q M E J E B D O Q R
```

"No SL̶Q̶Y̶, no Glory!"

Stealth Elf: *"_____ but Deadly!"*
Sunburn: *"Roast 'n' _____!"*
Terrafin: *"It's _____ Time!"*
Wham-Shell: *"_____ for the Mace!"*
Whirlwind: *"_____ of Fury!"*
Wrecking Ball: *"_____ 'n' Roll!"*
Zoo Lou: *"_____ Calls!"*
Zook: *"Locked and _____!"*

Trigger Happy

Do you think you have a good memory? Set a stopwatch and study the boxes below for one minute. Then turn to page 49 and answer the questions. Good luck!

MAGIC

MEMORY MASTERS

PART 1

TECH

SPOOKY SAMPLER

Issue 2,015
Price: 1 Petrified Darkness Crystal

NO.1 FOR EVIL GENIUSES

MINION MONTHLY

An A-Z of Evil
Your beginner's
guide to universal
domination

Creature
Control
How to train
your Fire Viper

Step-by-Step
Guide
Build your own
Evilizer

Minion
Management
101 ways to humiliate
your henchman

EXCLUSIVE!
Mother Knows Best
Kaos' Mom reveals her
deepest, darkest secrets

Top Terrors Tested • Latest Spells • Horror-scop

22

CROSSWORD OF DOOOM!

Can you survive our Evilized brain teaser?

Across

2. Kaos' Mom's right-hand monster (5,6)

7. Buccaneering baddies who get dizzy if they spin for too long (6,9)

10. The Lord of the Underworld (5, 9)

14. A giant Arkeyan robot once enslaved by Kaos (11)

15. Elves who follow the path of 12 down (4)

17. Watch out for these rocket-firing trolls (7,7)

18. A skeletal troll from beyond the grave (5,7)

19. Short, sinister and severely lacking in the hair department (4)

20. A minion that fires deadly spinning gears (4,9)

Down

1. The infernal heroes who defend Skylands from 12 down (3,10)

3. A floating mage that boosts your minions' might (3,5,4)

4. Pesky plants that spawn little green mouths-on-legs (6,4)

5. Puppet mistress (10)

6. A small, yellow, club-wielding minion (7)

8. An ancient spinning robot (7,3,5)

9. One-eyed wizard who can magnify any problem with his laser blasts (7, 9)

11. Chompies that go kaboom! (12)

12. The dark power behind all things evil (3,8)

13. Bomb-lobbing troll (4,4)

16. Butler to 19 across (10)

When you're done, write the letters in the shaded boxes here to reveal the name of one of evil's greatest enemies:

Listen to Mother

Glumshanks talks to Kaos' Mom about her wonderfully wretched career and bringing up everyone's favourite evil Portal Master.

GLUMSHANKS: Mistress, first of all I would like to thank you for taking time out of your busy schedule to talk to me.

KAOS' MOM: Anything for you, my dear Glumshanks. You know that. Besides, since I became trapped in this accursed mirror, I've a lot of time on my hands.

G: Yes, our readers may not know how that happened. Could you explain for those who may have missed the news?

KM: Of course. It was that dratted Tessa girl.

G: The one you'd kidnapped?

KM: The very same. There I was, happily blasting Skylanders to my heart's content, when she pushed the mirror to the ground. My magic bounced off the glass, hit me instead of the Skylander and, Dumshanks' your uncle, I found myself trapped for all eternity. Oh, the shame.

G: I'm sure Lord Kaos will rescue you.

KM: That little runt? I begged him to save his old mumsie, but the arrogant twerp was far too busy trying to take over Skylands.

G: By means of a highly convoluted plan that had little chance of succeeding?

KM: That's the one. Actually, he reminded me of his father at that point. Failure runs in the family.

G: Of course, you were a powerful Portal Master in your youth . . .

KM: I still am, you ignorant little worm. How dare you!

G: Yes, but now you're a powerful Portal Master trapped forever in an enchanted mirror.

KM: Good point, nicely made. Next question please . . .

G: Can you tell us anything about Lord Kaos' childhood?

KM: Really? You want to talk about him? Well, if we must. He was a vile baby and didn't improve with age. Always having tantrums and stealing his playmates' toys.

G: By 'playmates', you mean potatoes.

KM: Of course I mean potatoes. Do you really think I would let other children into the castle? Disgusting creatures, full of bad smells and constant demands. Kaos always wanted something. Attention. Food. Not to be locked in the dungeon with the dragon. Moan, moan, moan!

G: How did you juggle being an evil Portal Master with being a mother?

KM: I didn't bother, to be honest. Being evil was just more fun. Besides, I had you to look after him, Glumshanks.

G: You know, I don't remember actually applying for that job.

KM: It was either that, or be dropped into the middle of a sky-piranha storm.

G: I'm sure I chose the piranhas.

KM: You did. That's the joy of being evil. I can still remember your little green lip wobbling the first time I told you to change Kaos' nappy. Snigger. It's making me laugh just thinking about it. Ha ha!

G: So, what advice would you give to someone trying to get into the evil Portal Master business?

KM: Hee hee! You looked like you'd just been slapped in the face with a wet nauteloid. Bwa-ha-ha!

G: Riiight. I think we'll draw this interview to a close. Can someone get the Greebles to fetch the cover for the mirror, please?

KM: HA HA HA HA HAHAAAAAAAAAAAA AAAAAAAAAAAAAAAAAA!!!!

NEXT MONTH
Hektore the forgotten overlord: "No one even remembers my name. It's so embarrassing."

A is for Arkeyans

You've got to love the Arkeyans. Not only did they rule for thousands of years, enslaving every single race in Skylands, but they also built wonderfully despicable weapons. Saying that, it's a good job they were defeated by the first Skylanders or you'd never get the chance to conquer the known universe, would you?

B is for Blaze Brewers

Blaze Brewers are selling like hot flame-flowers this season. The ideal way to turn up the heat on horrid do-gooders.

Minion Monthly's

Don't know your Arkeyans from your Zeppelins?

Never fear. Your favourite magazine for megalomaniacs is here to help.

L is for Loose Cannons

Talk about heavy artillery. Trolls may not be as plentiful as they once were, but these shell-heads are proving more than a match for Skylanders in the field. Any future Lord (or Lady) of Skylands should set his (or her) targets on these super-shielded shooters.

M is for Magic Spell Punks

Your troops will be nothing to look at after they've been turned invisible by a Magic Spell Punk.

J is for Jellyfish

Once, Cyclops Sleetthrowers only lobbed shovelfuls of snow, which made them pretty much useless in the summer months. Thankfully, the one-eyed wonders have diversified. The Cyclops Queen recently discovered an eye-land entirely made of jellyfish – ideal ammo when the weather turns warmer!

K is for K-Bot Gloopgunners

Well, Kaos has done it again. His new line of Gloopgunners throw gunge from the top of their spring-loaded heads. The green goo was originally designed as a hair-restorer, but had the unfortunate side-effect of making your skin fall off. Nasty.

A-Z of Evil

C is for Chompies
An old favourite, Chompies now come in more flavours than ever. Chompy Pastepetals – that split into two when attacked – are currently on every would-be tyrant's wish list. Well, they do say two sets of razor-sharp teeth are better than one.

D is for Darkness
Ooh, isn't it just so dark and mysterious and just plain scary? The Darkness is the source of all evil in the universe. Where would we all be without it?

E is for Earth Geargolems
These heavy-hitters think with their fists and are happiest when repeatedly thumping the ground to create gigantic earthquakes.

H is for Hydra
Still believed to be lurking in the Outlands, the former arch-minion of Kaos has four fearsome heads. The Fire head breathed fire, the Water head spewed doomshark-infested floods, the Undead head blasted out laser beams and the Life head controlled swarms of deadly insects. Capable of destroying the Core of Light, the Hydra is fully house-trained.

F is for Fire Vipers
The must-have minions. Sand Serpents are OK for beginners and Two-Headed Spiders always draw the screams, but nothing says 'don't mess with me' better than having a rampant fire-breathing reptile watching your back. Just be careful – eight out of ten Fire Viper owners end up as toast.

I is for Ice Ogres
It's a little known fact that they are the most intelligent minions. Grade A geniuses, in fact. Unfortunately, they spend so long in sub-zero conditions that their brains have frozen, reducing the IQ of an average Ice Ogre to that of a particularly silly brick. A real pity.

G is for Greebles
There's a reason Greebles are cheap. They're rubbish. Actually, that's a little unfair to rubbish. The only reason you should consider hiring an army of Greebles is if you can't afford cyclopses. Or if you like losing. A lot.

N is for Knuckledusters (sort of)

These mini Arkeyan menaces replaced their right hands with cannons capable of blasting out red-hot plasma.

P is for Petrified Darkness

The rarest gem in all of Skylands. The Arkeyans used Petrified Darkness to fuel their war machines. Little did they know that it can be used to Evilize even the purest soul. Also looks good on rings, tiaras and cufflinks.

O is for the Outlands

Where no self-respecting follower of Darkness wants to be banished. A desolate, lonely, unforgiving place, devoid of any life to crush beneath your boot. On the plus side, there's little chance of being saddled by annoying neighbours who throw parties until all hours of the morning.

Z is for Zeppelins

Airships are for wimps. If you want to impress your enemies (and strike terror into their hearts), arrive in one of the latest zeppelins. And remember, when it comes to cannons, less is definitely not more. More is more. Always.

Y is for Yes-Men

All mega-villains need to have at least one toady to faun over them 24/7 and make them cocoa at the end of a hard day of being despicable. Warning: Never choose a Cyclops Mammoth as your lackey. They have a habit of ripping your head off, which is inconvenient in the extreme.

W is for Windbag Djinnis

Able to blow any airship off course, these calamitous clouds are also handy if you need to dry your washing in a hurry.

X is for Ex-Writer

Editor's note: Minion Monthly is in the process of looking for a new staff writer, after the author of this A-Z was fired following his failure to think of anything beginning with the letter X. When we say fired, of course we mean fired into the middle of a lava pit.

Q is for Qualifications

Gone are the days when any Tom, Dick or Count Moneybone could rock up and say they were an evil mastermind. These days you need the right qualifications. Apply today for the Minion Monthly University of Universal Domination. New courses include Minion Micro-Management, Evil Planning 101 and Advanced Cackling.

R is for Rockshooters

No one has ever seen a Grumblebum Rockshooter outside of its wooden gun-turret. Some say they hide away from the light as they are so appallingly ugly. Others claim it is because they're afraid of sunlight. The truth of the matter is that they're just really anti-social.

S is for Sheep Mage

A rising star in the Minion Monthly Hall of Fame, the Sheep Mage is able to transform himself, and anyone else, into a sheep. Brother to that appalling, enchilada-loving waste of space Chompy Mage, this horn-helmeted anti-hero is baaaaad to the bone.

U is for the Land of the Undead

Skylands' top holiday destinations for despots and evil dominators – and it's easy to see why. It boasts eternal night (perfect for topping up that pallid complexion) and the sound of screams at every turn. The only snag is that once you visit the Land of the Undead you are cursed to remain Undead yourself for all eternity. Still, it's a small price to pay for a wonderfully vile holiday.

T is for Trolls

Once the mainstay of any maniac, trolls are sadly becoming increasingly rare. Mainly because they keep blowing themselves up. Well, if you play with explosives you can expect to get your fingers blown off. And your arms. And your legs. And your head.

V is for Vortex Geargolems

An easy way of deploying minions in the midst of battle. Geargolems can either spawn reinforcements or drag enemies into the miniature black holes they store in their chests. Also good for vacuuming your evil lair.

WHAT KIND OF MINION ARE YOU?

START Which word best describes you?

- Speedy
- Strong
- Clever

Do you like being part of a crowd?
- Yes, the more the merrier
- No. Prefer it on my own!

What would you rather be?
- A pirate
- A wizard
- A robot

Do you like having a bath?
- No
- Yes

Do you do what you are told?
- Never
- Sometimes
- Always
- Love it

Are you a bit of a trickster?
- Yes
- No

Do you like flying?
- Not really

Which of Skylands' nastiest souls are you most like? Answer our devious questions to find out . . .

Do you like cold weather?

Yup!

Are you always hungry?

Yes → YOU ARE A **CHOMPY**

No → YOU ARE A **CYCLOPS**

No! I hate it

Are you a bit clumsy?

Yes → YOU ARE A **GREEBLE**

No → YOU ARE A **TROLL**

Magic or Technology?

Technology

Magic

Pointy ears or pointy hats?

Ears → YOU ARE A **DROW**

Hats → YOU ARE A **SPELL PUNK**

YOU ARE A **FIRE GEARGOLEM**

Do you like napping?

No

Yes

Are you the strong silent type?

Yes

No → YOU ARE AN **ARKEYAN**

DESIGN A MINION

Greetings, Portal Loser. It is I, KAOS. I hope you have enjoyed this Minion Monthly sampler. Actually, I don't care if you liked it or not – especially when I've heard you sniggering over the state of my minions. HOW DARE YOU! Think you could do better, eh? Think you could rival KAOS, the greatest minion master of all time?

FOOLISH FOOLS, I challenge you to design your very own minion. Draw it here if you dare! And don't forget, if I catch you laughing at me again, I'll feed you to my THREE-HEADED TERROR-ELEPHANTS OF DOOOM! YOU HAVE BEEN WARNED!

FIRE!

LASER EYES

KAOS STINK

Make sure you give your minion a name and at least one special ability!

THE PERFECT MATCH

Can you link the correct Skylander to the right description?

COUNTDOWN

DOOM STONE

BOOM JET

CHOP CHOP

DOUBLE TROUBLE

A

Element:	Earth
Battle cry:	"Another Smash Hit!"
Soul Gem Ability:	Spin the Tables
And another thing:	Was magically brought to life to serve an extremely lazy wizard

B

Element:	Magic
Battle cry:	"Boom-Shock-a-Laka!"
Soul Gem Ability:	Waterwalker
And another thing:	Became a Skylander after finding the super-rare Whispering Water Lily

C

Element:	Tech
Battle cry:	"I'm the Bomb!"
Soul Gem Ability:	Self-Destruct
And another thing:	Loses part of his memory every time he explodes! Why? He can't remember!

D

Element:	Undead
Battle cry:	"Slice and Dice!"
Soul Gem Ability:	Cursed Bone Brambler
And another thing:	Was created by an Arkeyan Lord who discovered how to combine Tech and Undead Elements

E

Element:	Air
Battle cry:	"Bombs Away!"
Soul Gem Ability:	Mach 2
And another thing:	This sky surfer hails from the distant Billowy Cloudplains

The Scarab Staff

Used by: Dune Bug

Where did it come from?
As a young beetle, Dune Bug used his father's magic staff to learn the secrets of a buried Arkeyan library. On the day when he received his own staff, the archive was attacked by the Sand Mages of Doom. Dune Bug defeated the mages and used the staff to hide the library and its mysteries forever.

What can it do?
Shoot powerful balls of energy.

Is that all?
No, it can also create magical dune balls that sweep enemies away.

Wacky

Check out some of the wildest weapons ever wielded by Skylands' finest

Swordfish

Used by: Rip Tide

Where did it come from?
Rip Tide acquired his trusty swordfish to boost his range of moves as a champion Aqua-Fighter. He became so good that, before long, even Eon had heard of his talents. When Kaos got wind of the Portal Master's plans to invite Rip Tide to become a Skylander, he sent a squad of Squidface Brutes to get in the way. Some chance. Rip Tide floored them with a Blubber Whale Wallop.

What can it do?
Slash and slice, although Rip Tide also likes sending it spinning towards his enemies.

Is that all?
Of course not! It can also turn into a swordshark or even a swordwhale. Rip Tide's blades have seen him through thick and fin.

Choose your weapon!
What are your favourite Skylander weapons? Jot down your top five here:

1.

2.

3.

4.

5.

The Malacostracan Mace

Used by: Wham-Shell

Where did it come from?
This Clam Kingdom heirloom had been handed down from one royal generation to the next – but when trolls invaded his father's underwater kingdom, Wham-Shell grabbed the ceremonial weapon and put it to good use, sending the marauders swimming back to the surface.

What can it do?
Crack anything – even the shell of the legendary Giant Sky-Lobster.

Is that all?
Are you kidding? It shoots energy-sapping starfish at foes. Take that, suckers!

Column Club

Used by: Doom Stone

Where did it come from?
Doom Stone first picked up his Column Club so he could learn the ancient art of Stone Fighting, just in case he ever had to protect his wizard master. It's lucky he did. When the wizard was kidnapped by his evil twin brother, the granite guardian used his self-taught skills to save the day.

What can it do?
Swing like a particularly heavy club. It's like being hit by a brick wall.

Is that all?
Nope. It can shatter into smaller pieces that smash enemies.

Weapons

Vac-Blaster

Used by: Jet-Vac

Where did it come from?
Master Eon gave Jet-Vac his powerful vacuum gun when the Sky Baron sacrificed his own wings to save a young mother and her children.

What can it do?
Blast bad guys with a stream of super-charged air.

Is that all?
Absolutely not. It can also suck enemies into its spinning blades.

Dance Off!
Not all Skylander weapons are deadly. The Groove Machine is a mystical beat box that hails from the Arkeyan age. Just hit the switch and enemies won't be able to attack, as they'll be too busy boogieing to kicking Arkeyan tunes.
Get down!

Mini Mix-Up
Can you match these Skylanders to their weapons?

A. Smolderdash   **B. Ignitor**   **C. Voodood**   **D. Chill**   **E. Trigger Happy**

1. Golden Pistols   **2. Axe Reaver**   **3. Ice Javelin**   **4. Scorching Blade**   **5. Flame Whip**

Water Load of Questions

Just how much do you know about Skylanders of the Water Element? Have you absorbed every scrap of information, or are you still a little wet behind the ears? Find out by diving head-first into this true or false quiz

1. Punk Shock saved her kingdom from underwater Chompies.

   TRUE ☐
   FALSE ☐

2. Wash Buckler hated his pirate life.

   TRUE ☐
   FALSE ☐

3. Zap is half water dragon, half electric eel.

   TRUE ☐
   FALSE ☐

4. Gill Grunt was once a pirate chief.

   TRUE ☐
   FALSE ☐

5. Wham-Shell is the son of Clam King Roland.

   TRUE ☐
   FALSE ☐

6. Rip Tide never won the legendary Rumble in the Reef contest.

   TRUE ☐
   FALSE ☐

7. Slam Bam always adds a little peppermint to his home-made snow cones.

   TRUE ☐
   FALSE ☐

8. Wham-Shell's Soul Gem Ability is called Carapace Plating.

   TRUE ☐
   FALSE ☐

9. Thumpback's Sidekick is called Shrimpback.

   TRUE ☐
   FALSE ☐

10. Chill was the Captain of the Snow Queen's Guard.

TRUE ☐
FALSE ☐

11. Zap is a friend to dolphins everywhere.

TRUE ☐
FALSE ☐

12. Freeze Blade was born in the Great Lava Lakes.

TRUE ☐
FALSE ☐

13. Giant Thumpback served under the evil pirate Captain Frightbeard.

TRUE ☐
FALSE ☐

14. Wash Buckler is a Scuttlefish.

TRUE ☐
FALSE ☐

15. Slam Bam used to have six arms, but two snapped off when he was frozen by an Ice Spell Punk.

TRUE ☐
FALSE ☐

16. Punk Shock is a member of the Wonderous Waters royal family.

TRUE ☐
FALSE ☐

17. Rip Tide's battle cry is "Fear the Fin!"

TRUE ☐
FALSE ☐

18. Chill's greatest enemy is the Narwhal.

TRUE ☐
FALSE ☐

19. Freeze Blade throws icy chakrams.

TRUE ☐
FALSE ☐

20. The Water Giant turned his back on evil when he was defeated by Terrafin.

TRUE ☐
FALSE ☐

ZOO LOU'S WORDQUEST

Can you find a path through the grid using all the words listed below? Use the last letter of the first word to start the next one — move up, down or sideways but never diagonally. Zoo Lou has found the first one to start you off.

EARTH	ERUPTOR	NIGHT SHIFT	DUFF	SPELL PUNK	~~FLYNN~~	SHARPFIN
SWAP FORCE	LIGHTNING ROD	OCCULOUS	TWISTY TUNNELS	FLAVIUS	HUGO	KAOS
ELEMENTAL GATE	POWER PODS	NINJINI	SWARM	NOODLES	SHEEP	RUMBLETOWN
SUGARBATS	ORACLE	SPYRO	EYE-SMALL	SOUL GEMS	ICE OGRE	MAGIC

F	N	N	I	F	T	W	I	S	T	U	E	L	S	P	E
L	Y	S	G	I	O	R	Y	T	Y	N	N	U	P	L	L
M	S	E	H	H	R	O	P	S	O	A	K	N	R	U	M
A	L	Y	T	S	A	C	L	E	R	U	P	T	O	M	B
I	L	E	R	G	C	I	N	I	J	N	I	N	T	E	L
G	H	T	N	O	E	H	D	U	F	F	L	W	O	S	U
U	O	L	I	N	G	R	O	S	E	L	A	V	I	U	G
S	W	U	C	O	N	E	B	O	U	D	O	R	E	W	A
R	A	R	C	A	T	M	E	G	L	O	O	P	O	O	R
M	M	G	O	L	G	E	M	S	W	I	N	S	D	P	B
A	C	U	R	A	A	L	R	O	A	F	O	H	E	E	A
G	I	H	T	E	T	E	C	F	P	P	R	.	A	H	S	T

When you're finished, you should be left with ten letters that you didn't use.
Rearrange them to form the name of another Life Skylander.

_ _ _ _ _ _ _ _ _ _

40

A DAY IN THE LIFE OF Cynder

8am
Today did not start well. There was a call for help from Woodburrow. The Chompy Mage had seeded the entire town with Chompy Pods. There were Chompy Rustbuds all over the place. I raced over to the Portal, only to be tripped by one of Wash Buckler's stupid tentacles. Trigger Happy obviously thought it was one of the funniest things he'd ever seen. He wasn't laughing when I butted him halfway across the ruins. While I was at it I also gave Wash Buckler a short, sharp, shock to teach him not to leave his tentacles lying around.

10am
Back at the Ruins. Those Chompies were no problem at all. Turns out the Chompy Mage just wanted to show them off to the old Chieftess. Apparently, they had been friends when they were younger. See, this is why friendships can be a pain in the butt. Talking of which, I treated the Chompy Mage's rear end to a few thousand volts when no one was looking. Deserves everything he gets, that one. Besides, no one was looking.

10.05am
Turns out someone was looking. Just got a right old ticking off from Spyro. Apparently Skylanders don't blast people for making an honest mistake. Honest? The Chompy Mage? You're kidding, right?

12pm
Just when I thought today couldn't get any worse – there's bright sunshine. Awful. What's a girl got to do to get some bad weather around here?

2pm
Back in action. Kaos was trying out his new Terrible Terrifying Trees of Terror spell. It was supposed to transform all the Mabu on Pirate Plateau into, you guessed it, trees. Instead it transformed all the trees into Mabu. Absolute madness. Even I had to feel sorry for all the squirrels that suddenly found themselves living in furry little Mabu instead of majestic oaks. We sent Kaos packing, although Lightning Rod took all the credit as usual. I made sure I told him what I thought of that!

4pm
Hmmm. Just walked into the Portal room to find Spyro, Rod, Wash Buckler and Trig deep in conversation. They all shut up when they saw me. Typical. Just because a dragon speaks her mind – and electrocutes one or two people . . .

5pm
Really not happy. Eon has sent me on a right wild sheep chase. Portalled me over to the Chocolate Tundra to track down the Golden Kangarat Hat. There's nothing there, except for miles and miles of sticky chocolate dunes. Someone is going to get a haunting when I get home.

5.10pm
Something's wrong. Just got back to the Ruins and no one's here. Also, it's cloudy. Really cloudy. It's never stormy this near the Core of Light. What's happened?

5.20pm
I've got a bad feeling about this. Have just found Wash Buckler's hat on the floor. And there's one of Trigger Happy's pistols. Oh no. There's a giant Chompy Pod, right by the Ruins. That's it. I'm going in.

6pm
Gah, they hooked me like a Gillman. It wasn't Chompies inside the Chompy Pod. It was Spyro, Trig and the rest. Was about to blast the pesky plant when they jumped out and shouted 'surprise!'. They've been planning my surprise hatchday party for weeks! They borrowed a dormant pod off the Chompy Mage, and Lightning Rod even gathered some low-lying cloud to make it nice and gloomy. My friends are great! Going to try to be a little more patient with them. Best. Day. Ever.

6.05pm
Just tripped over Wrecking Ball's tongue! Wait till I get my claws on that little grub . . .

HEAD TO HEAD

CHOP CHOP VS.

ROUND 1:
CHILLING NAME

CHOP CHOP	GRIM CREEPER

ROUND 2:
BALEFUL BATTLE CRY

"Slice and Dice!"	"Your Time is Up!"

ROUND 3:
AWFUL APPEARANCE

A walking skeleton warrior who hides his face behind a foreboding mask.	A giggling, glowing ghoul dressed from head to toe in haunted armour.

ROUND 4:
TERRIBLE TRAINING

Trained at the arcane Arkeyan military academy.	Trained at the Grim Acres School for Ghost Wrangling.

ROUND 5:
OMINOUS ORIGINS

Chop Chop was the result of a crazy experiment to fuse the power of the Tech and Undead Elements. The spine-chilling soldier survived the fall of the Arkeyan Empire and clambered to the surface, searching for new orders. He trudged from island to island until he came across Master Eon, and was recruited as a Skylander.

Turned away by the Scaremaster of Grim Acres for not being scary enough, Grim Creeper proved himself when the other pupils turned and fled from a phantom invasion. Grim stood his ground and sliced the spooks into smithereens. Now, years later, he is recognized as the greatest reaper to ever swing a scythe.

It's the clash of the terrors. Who is scarier – the Arkeyan elite guard or the spooky ghost reaper? You decide. Tick your winner in every round to see who's made of the fright stuff!

GRIM CREEPER

ROUND 6:
WEIRD WEAPON

Twin Arkeyan Blades, sharp enough to slice a Trog hair in two.	A spectral scythe capable of slashing through sinister spirits.

ROUND 7:
ALARMING ABILITY

Summons bony brambles from the very depths of the earth. One scratch and you're history.	Splits into a spectral ghost form, while his enchanted armour keeps fighting.

ROTTEN RESULT
Which Undead Skylander will you crown as your creepy champion? Add up your supernatural scores below.

Chop Chop	/7	Grim Creeper	/7

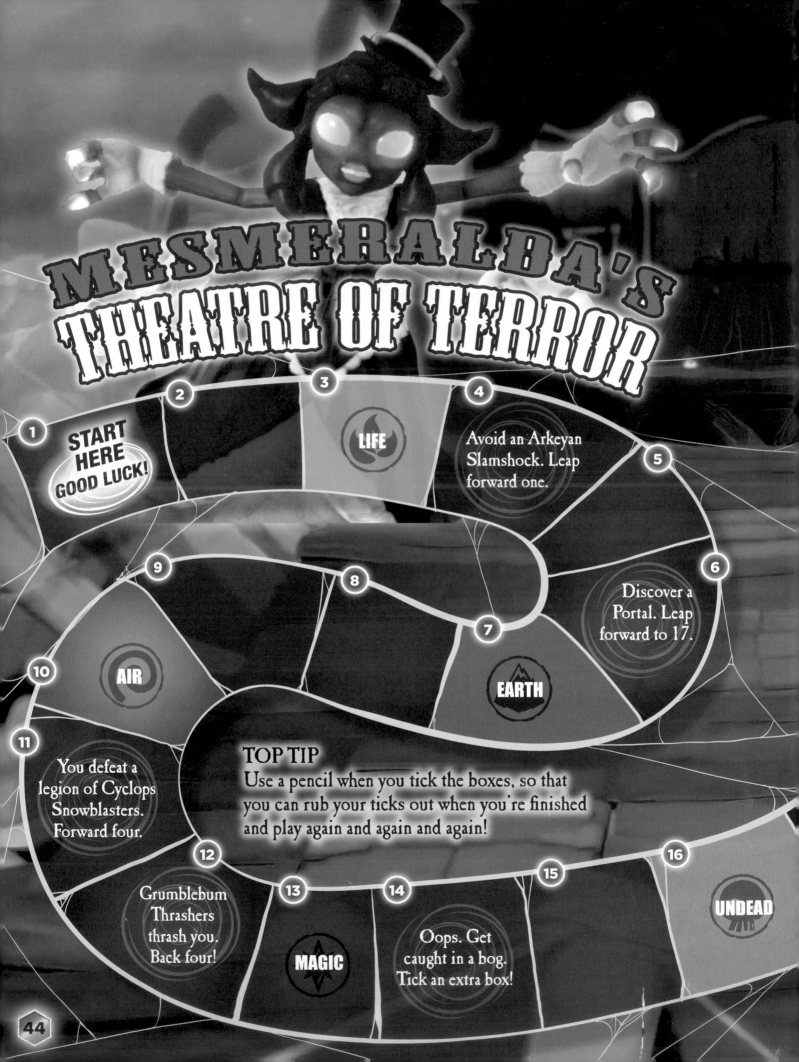

MESMERALDA'S THEATRE OF TERROR

1 START HERE GOOD LUCK!

2

3 LIFE

4 Avoid an Arkeyan Slamshock. Leap forward one.

5

6 Discover a Portal. Leap forward to 17.

7 EARTH

8

9

10 AIR

11 You defeat a legion of Cyclops Snowblasters. Forward four.

TOP TIP
Use a pencil when you tick the boxes, so that you can rub your ticks out when you're finished and play again and again and again!

12 Grumblebum Thrashers thrash you. Back four!

13 MAGIC

14 Oops. Get caught in a bog. Tick an extra box!

15

16 UNDEAD

Oh no! You've been caught in Mesmeralda's clutches. The marionette mistress wants to turn you into one of her puppet slaves. Escape from her theatre while you can!

How to play!
1. This is a game for one, but can also be played by two or more. It's up to you.
2. Play using one of your Skylanders figurines and a die.
3. Roll the die and move your Skylander forward, following the instructions on the board.
4. Every time you roll the die, tick one of the boxes. If you've ticked them all before you reach the end, you've lost and have been transformed into one of Mesmeralda's puppets. It's curtains for you!

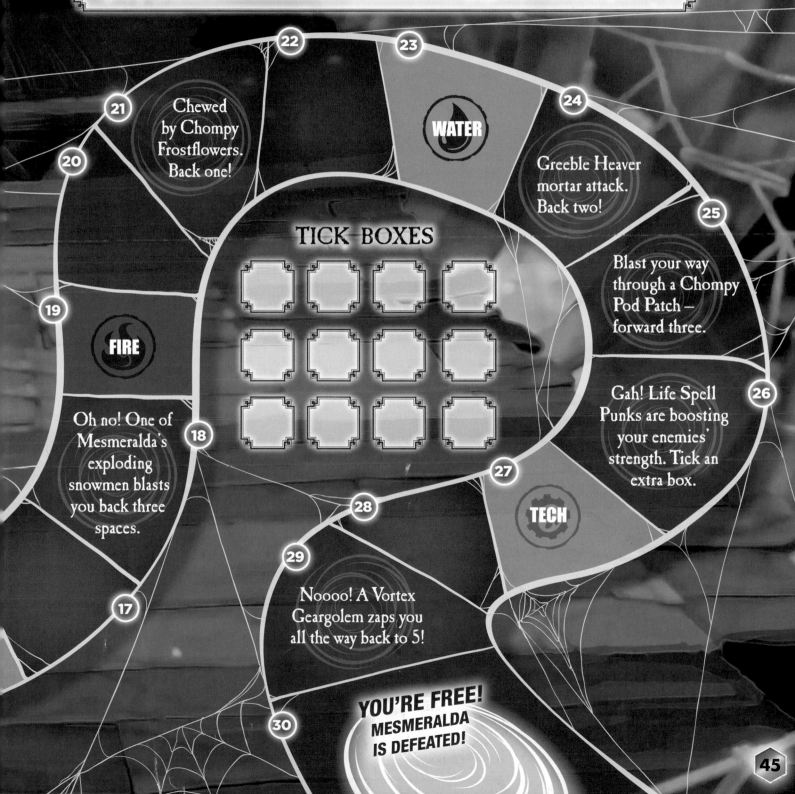

21 Chewed by Chompy Frostflowers. Back one!

24 Greeble Heaver mortar attack. Back two!

TICK BOXES

25 Blast your way through a Chompy Pod Patch – forward three.

19 FIRE

26 Gah! Life Spell Punks are boosting your enemies' strength. Tick an extra box.

18 Oh no! One of Mesmeralda's exploding snowmen blasts you back three spaces.

27 TECH

29 Noooo! A Vortex Geargolem zaps you all the way back to 5!

YOU'RE FREE!
MESMERALDA IS DEFEATED!

Make a Chompy Hat

Hats are a big deal in Skylands. Especially if you have a big head. Why not create your own Chompy headgear? It's what every stylish Skylander is wearing this season!

You will need:

- Some old newspaper
- A balloon
- Acrylic or poster paints
- Craft paper
- Card
- PVA or white glue
- A paintbrush

1. Blow up the balloon until it's a little bit bigger than your head. Give it lots of puff!

2. Tear your newspaper into strips.

3. Make papier mache paste by mixing two parts white glue with one part water (you can always ask an adult to help with this bit!).

4. Dip your paper strips into the paste, letting them absorb the moisture. Now lay the paper on the top of the balloon, smoothing out the paper with a paintbrush. Repeat the process until the top half of the balloon is completely covered.

5. Make two or three more layers, then leave the entire thing to dry for two or three days.

6. When it's dry, pop the balloon. You'll be left with your hat shape!

Top Tip
Stand the balloon in a bowl or small bucket while sticking on the papier mache.

7. Trim the edges of your hat so it's nice and straight.

8. Make newspaper pulp by mixing small squares of newspaper into the papier mache paste and adding a small amount of PVA glue.

9. Use the newspaper pulp to build up the shape of the Chompy's mouth on the front of the hat. Then, cover the mouth with strips of paper and PVA glue to give it a smooth finish.

10. Now use the newspaper pulp again to form the shape of the Chompy's teeth, again covering with paper and PVA glue for a smooth finish. Now leave to dry.

11. Once it's all dry, it's time to paint your hat!

12. Use your craft paper and card to create eyes on stalks, and little Chompy arms. Stick them to your hat.

13. Lastly, put your finished creation on your head, and you're done. Chomp chomp!

Try different colours for different Chompies – yellow for a Pastepetal, red and yellow for a Blitzbloom or icy blue for a Frostflower!

HIDE AND SNEAK!

Stealth Elf is trapped in the middle of Kaos' LABYRINTH OF DEADLY DOOM! Can you help her find the right exit, avoiding his Evilized minions?

Did you know?

Stealth Elf's earliest memory is a wild and woolly dream about stampeding sheep. What a nightmare!

MEMORY MASTERS PART 2

It's time to answer those questions about page 20. How much can you remember without peeking?

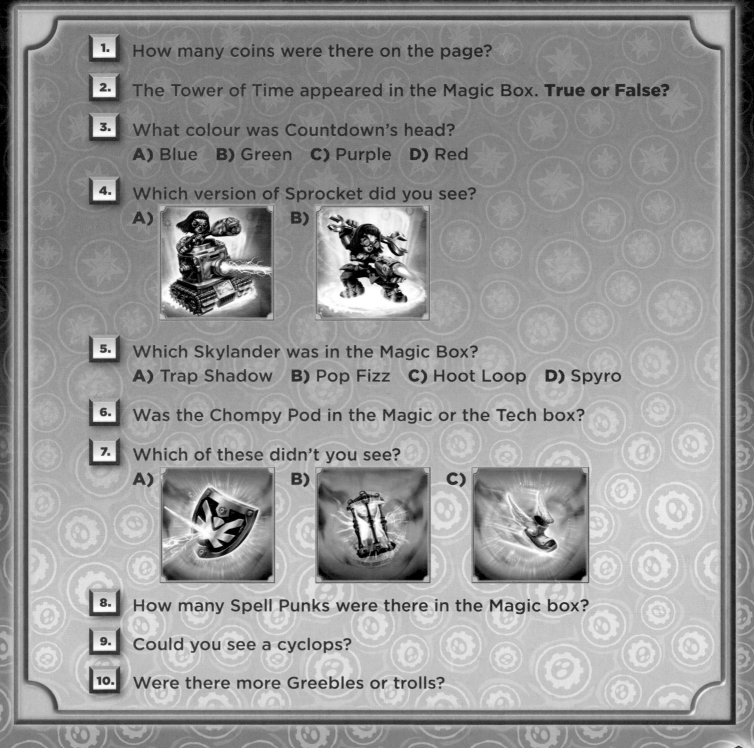

1. How many coins were there on the page?

2. The Tower of Time appeared in the Magic Box. **True or False?**

3. What colour was Countdown's head?
A) Blue   **B)** Green   **C)** Purple   **D)** Red

4. Which version of Sprocket did you see?
A)   **B)**

5. Which Skylander was in the Magic Box?
A) Trap Shadow   **B)** Pop Fizz   **C)** Hoot Loop   **D)** Spyro

6. Was the Chompy Pod in the Magic or the Tech box?

7. Which of these didn't you see?
A)   **B)**   **C)**

8. How many Spell Punks were there in the Magic box?

9. Could you see a cyclops?

10. Were there more Greebles or trolls?

HEAD GAMES

by Onk Beakman

Continued from page 13!

PART TWO: FACES OF EVIL

"No!" the Ents wailed, as Shellshock cackled uncontrollably. "Spyro's been Evilized!"

"Shouldn't we be running?" Flynn asked, releasing the last of the explorers from their restraints.

"Don't worry," insisted Wind-Up. "Shellshock hasn't won yet."

"Vot are you talking about?" the crab shrieked with laughter. "Spyro is vun of us now. He serves the Darkness. As Lordenzie Kaos says, you are doomed!"

In the centre of the clearing, Spyro's spines bristled, arcane energies flowing over his darkening scales.

"More!" he roared, fangs bared. "Give me all you've got!"

"No!" Shellshock cried out as the crystals on the staff began to crack. "It is too much. Too much power!"

"Never too much," Spyro growled, flapping his ebony wings and rising from the ground. His voice wasn't one his friends even recognized any more. It was deeper, with an edge they'd never heard before – like something from the depths of a nightmare.

Shellshock scuttled back a few paces as the crystals shattered. "I do not understand," he squealed. "Vot is happening?"

Spyro – or Dark Spyro, as he was now – grinned a hideous grin. "Your master tried to turn me a long time ago, flooding my body with pure Darkness."

"Yeah," chipped in Scorp, his claws full of Sting Balls. "But Kaos found out that even the Darkness can't control Spyro."

Crackling boxing gloves appeared in Wind-Up's claws. "Spyro controlled it!"

"Zat is not possible," Shellshock spluttered.

Dark Spyro's eyes flashed red. "Funny, that's what Kaos said when I did this!"

The dragon roared, dark purple flames gushing from his open jaws, smothering the trees. One by one, the unnatural plants shattered, the purple gems exploding like fireworks.

"Noooo!" Shellshock wailed. "The Petrified Darkness! Stop him someone! Stop him now!"

But the crab's Greeble army was busy being punched and pummelled by Wind-Up and Scorp. Orbs were flying, stings were striking and oversized boxing gloves were connecting with feeble Greeble chins.

Shellshock's beady eyes fell upon Flynn, who was hurriedly herding the last remaining Ents out of the chamber to safety. The crab glanced at his shattered staff and back at the pilot, his mandibles twisting into a horrid leer. "Just enough power left . . ."

He swung the staff around and fired.

***

"That's it, Spyro," Wind-Up shouted up at their transformed friend. "You're doing it!"

"But will he be able to stop?" hissed Scorp, slamming his stinger into the ground to create shockwaves that sent the remaining Greebles flying. The Skylanders shared a knowing look. Spyro's ability to filter dark energies was impressive, but they all secretly wondered if becoming Dark Spyro would one day prove too much for him.

"Don't worry about him," growled a voice from behind them. "Worry about me!"

They span around to see a massive figure looming over them.

"Flynn," Wind-Up gasped. "What's happened to you?"

"Ain't it obvious?" Scorp rumbled, bracing for an attack. "He's been Evilized!"

The pilot laughed, throwing back his head. His big head. His really big head. It was five times its normal size, and crowned with glistening crystals of Darkness.

"I always told you I was a big deal," Evilized Flynn sneered. "BOOM!"

The air in front of Flynn's gigantic face exploded, sending Dark Spyro crashing to the ground. His dark energies almost exhausted, Spyro's scales had almost returned to their natural shade.

"I don't believe it," he gasped. "Flynn's 'booms' actually go —"

BOOM!

Another explosion shook the cave. Dust tumbled from the high ceiling as Evilized Flynn puffed out his chest.

"Everything changes," he thundered, his hands on his hips. "No more ferrying people from island to island. No more taking orders from stupid passengers. Now I'm the biggest and best. BOOM! BOOM! BOOM!"

Scorp was thrown across the cavern by the blast, Spyro only narrowly missing falling rocks dislodged by the explosions.

"Watch it, Flynn," Scorp coughed, choking on the dust. "You'll have the roof down."

"That's it!" exclaimed Wind-Up, who had been watching Shellshock collecting the remaining crystals. "Don't listen to them, Flynn," the clockwork Skylander shouted up. "Keep going. You're better than ever. Absolutely brilliant!"

Evilized Flynn beamed. "I am, aren't I?"

"Handsome. Charming," Wind-Up waggled his metal eyebrows. "A wow with the ladies."

"What are you doing?" Scorp barked, but Spyro had realized what Wind-Up was up to.

"Look at his head," Spyro hissed. "It's growing!"

It was true. With every compliment, Evilized Flynn's head was swelling, doubling in size. It was already nearly touching the ceiling.

"Wind-Up's right," Spyro joined in. "No one flies like you."

"And there's definitely no one who lands like you!" Scorp added quickly.

"No one protects Skylands like you!" shouted Wind-Up.

"I am pretty wonderful," Evilized Flynn commented, a dreamy look passing over his Evilized features. "Everyone says so."

The crystals on his head scraped across the ceiling.

"We're not the heroes, Flynn," shouted Spyro, struggling to be heard over the sound of the crystals grinding against rock, "you are. The greatest hero in all of Skylands."

That did it. Flynn's head expanded so fast that it smashed straight into the roof, the crystals on his super-sized bonce shattering as they pushed through to sunlight.

"Come on," said Spyro, grabbing Wind-Up and Scorp as the entire place started to cave in. "Let's fly!"

***

"Woah, what happened?" Flynn moaned, his now normal-sized head in his hands. The pilot had returned to normal as soon as the crystals had shattered. "It feels like someone dropped a cave on me."

"No, that's what happened to Shellshock," whirred Wind-Up happily. "He's down there somewhere, buried with hundreds of smashed crystals."

"So, we saved the day?" Flynn said, looking up at the Skylanders."

"No," chuckled Scorp. "You did!"

"Me?"

"With a little help from your friends," grinned Spyro.

"That's all right then," Flynn said, attempting a lopsided smile. "You know me, I don't like to boast!"

THE END

Spy Rise's Spy School

Could you become a top secret Spylander? Kaos has stolen a powerful Arkeyan artefact known as the Heart of Horrendous Horrors. Can you help Spy Rise solve these mind-bending mysteries and discover where the evil Portal Master has hidden the ancient weapon of doooom?

1. FOLLOW THAT ARTEFACT

G	A	R	W	P	C	E	D	T	Y	A	S	H	A	O	L	F	A
F	E	S	A	O	F	E	S	O	M	D	V	R	L	S	I	N	K
N	R	S	S	T	Y	N	O	S	J	O	I	N	F	A	C	Y	S
Z	D	O	N	R	R	V	C	N	R	A	U	B	T	R	Y	D	N

Match the graph to the grid above to find the last known location of the Heart of Horrendous Horrors.

Write it below when you've cracked the code!

2. ODD ONE OUT

Well done! You've found the door to Kaos' secret stash. To open it you need to work out which of these heroes is the odd one out.

3. MINION MASH-UP!

You've got into the secret vault, but you need to battle through Kaos' minions. Unscramble their names to discover which enemies you'll have to fight.

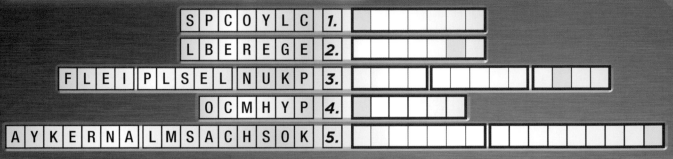

S P C O Y L C	1.	
L B E R E G E	2.	
F L E I P L S E L N U K P	3.	
O C M H Y P	4.	
A Y K E R N A L M S A C H S O K	5.	

4. BEAT THE BOSS

Uh-oh! Kaos has left one of Skylands' finest criminal minds in charge of the vault. Find out who it is by writing down the letters in the blue squares of the Minion Mash-Up grid.

5. FINAL BATTLE

You've spotted the Heart of Horrendous Horrors. You just need to blast those three Arkeyan warriors standing guard. On the grid below are four points Spy Rise can reach to fire his leg lasers from. Which three points should he fire from so that he can take out the bad guys but leave Slam Bam standing? Remember, those lasers can bounce off walls!

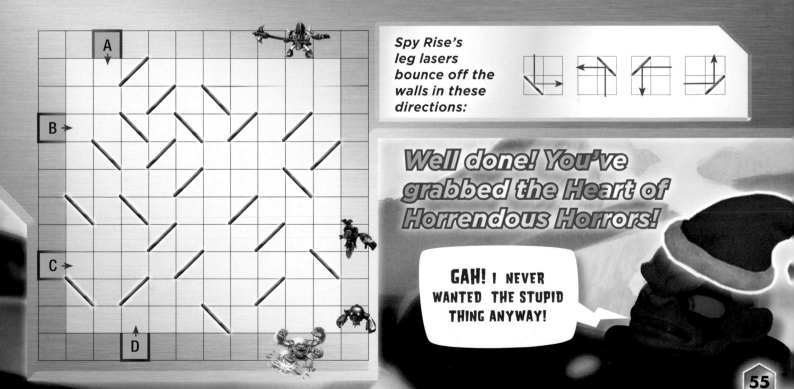

Spy Rise's leg lasers bounce off the walls in these directions:

Well done! You've grabbed the Heart of Horrendous Horrors!

GAH! I NEVER WANTED THE STUPID THING ANYWAY!

55

Five minutes with Fryno!

The red-hot road hog reveals all!

FIRE or WATER?
Do I even have to answer that?

MASTER EON or LORD KAOS?
No contest! Eon rocks, even for an old dude. As for Kaos – if that loser comes anywhere near me he won't need a Portal. I'll send him flying back to his fortress head-first!

SPORT or SNOOZE?
Sport! You snooze, you lose!

THE SKYLANDERS or THE BLAZING BIKER BRIGADE?
Skylanders! I haven't rode with the B.B.B. ever since I found out they were a bunch of crooks. **They** found out why you should never make me angry!

FAST or SLOW?
The faster the better!

MABU or ENTS?
The Ents are made of wood, right? Not a good idea. We'd probably get on like a house on fire, which could be a problem.

LEGENDARY TREASURE or HATS?
Hats every time! I can wear two – one on my head and the other on my horn! Stylish or what?

FLYNN or HUGO?
Flynn. The guy may be full of hot air, but he shares my need for speed!

BIKE or BOAT?
What is it with you and water? I'm happiest on two wheels, burning rubber – or anything else, for that matter.

TROLL or GREEBLE
Neither!

ENCHILADAS or PIZZA?
Enchiladas – as long as they're packed with chillies and covered in chilli sauce and come with a side order of extra chillies. I like my food hot, hot, hot!

ICE CREAM SUNDAE or SHEEP WOOL DESSERT?
Ice cream? Me? You're getting me fired up now. Unless you can get chilli ice cream. Do they make that?

Slobber the Difference

Spell Punks have been messing with this picture of Slobber Tooth. Can you find eight differences between the two scenes?

? Did you know?

When Slobber Tooth woke from hibernation, Kaos tried to recruit him as a minion. Some chance! Kaos found himself clobbered halfway across Skylands.

ROUND 1
Easy Peasy!

1. Flynn's ship is called the:
a) Dread-Ship
b) Dread-Boat
c) Dread-Yacht

2. What is the name of the mountain that spreads magic all over Skylands?
a) Mount Thunderstorm
b) Mount Cloudbreak
c) Mount Tempest

3. What Element does Wind-Up belong to?
a) Tech
b) Life
c) Magic

4. Tessa is the chieftess of which town?
a) Woodworm
b) Woodhampton
c) Woodburrow

5. Which of these Skylanders isn't a member of the SWAP Force?

a) b) c) d)

TERRAFIN'S KNOCKOUT CHALLENGE

ROUND 2 Getting Harder!

6. What is the name of Tessa's giant bird?
a) Claws
b) Feathers
c) Whiskers

7. The Freebots appear in which Skylanders game?
a) Skylanders Spyro's Adventure
b) Skylanders Giants
c) Skylanders SWAP Force

8. Can you identify this minion from its silhouette? Is it a:
a) Twistpick Cyclops
b) Cadet Crasher
c) Greeble Screwball

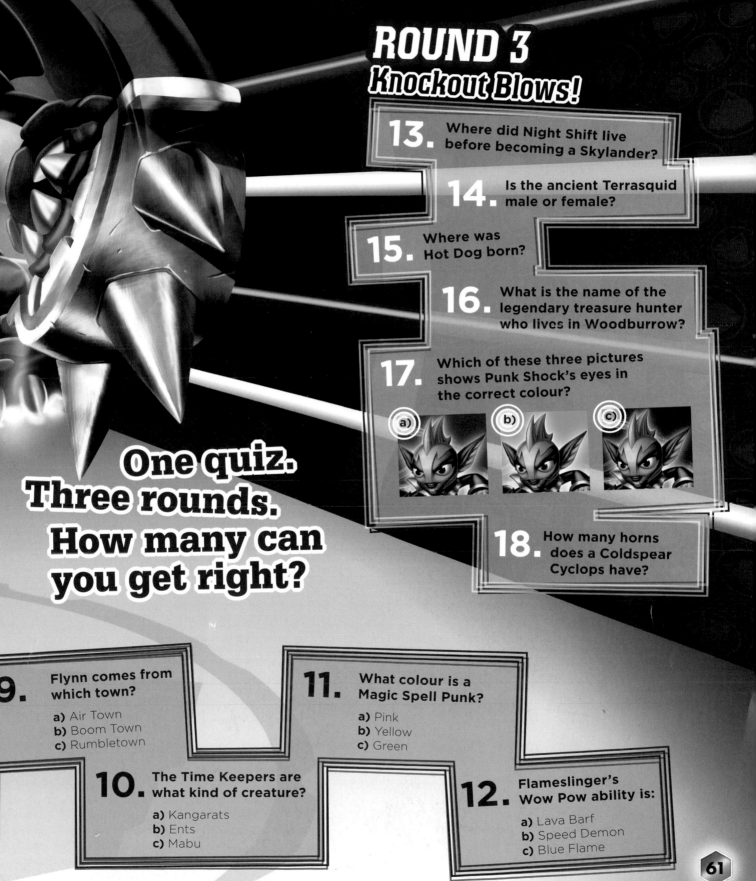

ROUND 3
Knockout Blows!

13. Where did Night Shift live before becoming a Skylander?

14. Is the ancient Terrasquid male or female?

15. Where was Hot Dog born?

16. What is the name of the legendary treasure hunter who lives in Woodburrow?

17. Which of these three pictures shows Punk Shock's eyes in the correct colour?

a)   b)   c)

18. How many horns does a Coldspear Cyclops have?

One quiz. Three rounds. How many can you get right?

9. Flynn comes from which town?
a) Air Town
b) Boom Town
c) Rumbletown

10. The Time Keepers are what kind of creature?
a) Kangarats
b) Ents
c) Mabu

11. What colour is a Magic Spell Punk?
a) Pink
b) Yellow
c) Green

12. Flameslinger's Wow Pow ability is:
a) Lava Barf
b) Speed Demon
c) Blue Flame

Answers

Page 5 – *Hat Hunt*

Page 39

Page 46

Page 25

Page 16

Page 55

Page 18–19: *Battle Cry Bonanaza*

Blast Zone: Furious
Bouncer: Wheel
Bumble Blast: Perfect
Camo: Fruit
Chill: Cool
Chop Chop: Slice
Cynder: Lightning
Drobot: Destroy
Dune Bug: Beetle
Eruptor: Born
Freeze Blade: Keeping
Flashwing: Blinded
Free Ranger: Storm
Fright Rider: Spear
Ghost Roaster: Chain
Gill Grunt: Fear
Hot Dog: Spot
Magna Charge: Attract
Ninjini: Wishes
Pop Fizz: Motion
Pop Thorn: Straight
Prism Break: Supreme
Roller Brawl: Roll
Scorp: Sting
Scratch: Luck
Slam Bam: Dangerous
Slobber Tooth: Clobber
Smolderdash: Glory
Spy Rise: Classified
Spyro: Fired
Stealth Elf: Silent
Sunburn: Toast
Terrafin: Feeding
Trigger Happy: Gold
Wham-Shell: Brace
Whirlwind: Twists
Wrecking Ball: Wreck
Zoo Lou: Nature
Zook: Loaded

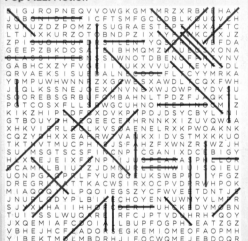

Page 22: *Crossword of Dooom!*

MASTER EON is the name in the shaded boxes.

Page 35: *The Perfect Match*

A – Doom Stone
B – Double Trouble
C – Countdown
D – Chop Chop
E – Boom Jet

Page 37: *Mini Mix-Up*

A. 5 B. 4 C. 2 D. 3 E. 1

Pages 38–39: *Water Load of Questions*

1. False. It was Snow Trolls.
2. True. He convinced his crew to turn good!
3. False. He's 100% water dragon but was raised by eels.
4. False. He was a Gillman Marine
5. True. He was a wise underwater ruler.
6. False. Are you kidding? He won every year!
7. True. It's his secret ingredient.
8. True. It gives him unbreakable armor.
9. False. He's called Thumpling.
10. True. Until she lost the Queen to marauding cyclopses.
11. False. They don't like the way he electrocutes their waters.
12. False. He comes from the Frozen Wastelands of Vesh.
13. True. He was once a member of the Phantom Tide crew.
14. False. He's a Mermasquid.
15. False. He's always had four, just like other yetis.
16. True. Although she hated royal life.
17. False. It's "Go Fish!"
18. False. They're best buddies.
19. True. They're as sharp as an icicle.
20. False. Thumpback was never evil. He only became a pirate so he could go fishing.

Page 40: *Zoo Lou's Wordquest*

The other Life Skylander is SHROOMBOOM.

Page 48: *Hide and Sneak*

Page 49: *Memory Masters*

1. 4
2. True
3. D
4. B
5. C
6. Tech
7. A
8. 3
9. No
10. There were more Greebles.

Pages 54–55: *Spy Rise's Spy School*

1. FOLLOW THAT ARTEFACT
Frostfest Mountains

2. ODD ONE OUT
Hot Head is the odd one out because he is a Giant.

3. MINION MASH-UP

1. CYCLOPS
2. GREEBLE
3. LIFE SPELL PUNK
4. CHOMPY
5. ARKEYAN SLAMSHOCK

4. BEAT THE BOSS
Cluck

5. FINAL BATTLE
Shoot leg lasers from A, B and D to destroy Arkeyan warriors:

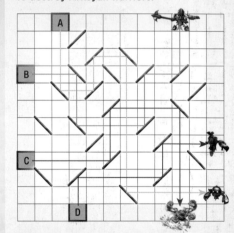

Pages 59: *Slobber the Difference*

Pages 60–61: *Terrafin's Knockout Challenge*

1. C
2. B
3. A
4. C
5. C
6. C
7. B
8. C
9. B
10. A
11. A
12. B
13. The Batcrypt Mountains
14. Female
15. The Popcorn Volcano
16. Tibbet
17. C
18. Two